REFLECTIONS
FOR
LENT 2015

Church House Publishing
Church House
Great Smith Street
London SW1P 3AZ

ISBN 978 0 7151 4460 2

Published 2014 by Church House Publishing
Copyright © The Archbishops' Council 2014

The opinions expressed in this book are those of the
authors and do not necessarily reflect the official policy of
the General Synod or The Archbishops' Council of the
Church of England.

Liturgical editor: Peter Moger
Series editor: Hugh Hillyard-Parker
Designed and typeset by Hugh Hillyard-Parker
Copy edited by: Ros Connelly
Printed by CPI Group (UK) Ltd, Croydon, CR0 4YY

What do you think of *Reflections for Daily Prayer*?

We'd love to hear from you – simply email us at

publishing@churchofengland.org

or write to us at

Church House Publishing, Church House,
Great Smith Street, London SW1P 3AZ.

Visit **www.dailyprayer.org.uk** for more
information on the *Reflections* series, ordering
and subscriptions.

REFLECTIONS
FOR
LENT

18 February – 4 April 2015

MALCOLM GUITE
BEN QUASH
FRANCES WARD
LUCY WINKETT

with an introduction by SAMUEL WELLS

Contents

About the authors

Stephen Cottrell is the Bishop of Chelmsford. Before this he was Bishop of Reading and has worked in parishes in London, Chichester, and Huddersfield and as Pastor of Peterborough Cathedral. He is a well-known writer and speaker on evangelism, spirituality and catechesis. His best-selling *How to Pray* (CHP) and *How to Live* (CHP) have recently been reissued.

Malcolm Guite, the Chaplain of Girton College Cambridge, is a poet and singer–songwriter, and is the author of *What do Christians Believe?* (Granta 2006), *Faith Hope and Poetry* (Ashgate 2010), *Sounding the Seasons; Seventy Sonnets for the Christian Year* (Canterbury 2012) and *The Singing Bowl* (Canterbury 2013).

John Pritchard has recently retired as Bishop of Oxford. Prior to that he has been Bishop of Jarrow, Archdeacon of Canterbury and Warden of Cranmer Hall, Durham. His only ambition was to be a vicar, which he was in Taunton for eight happy years. He enjoys armchair sport, walking, reading, music, theatre and recovering.

Ben Quash has been Professor of Christianity and the Arts at King's College London since 2007, and is Director of the Centre for Arts and the Sacred at King's (ASK). Prior to that he was Dean and Fellow of Peterhouse, Cambridge. He runs a collaborative MA in Christianity and the Arts with the National Gallery in London, and is also Canon Theologian of both Coventry and Bradford Cathedrals.

Frances Ward has been Dean of St Edmundsbury in the county of Suffolk since 2010. Previously she was a Residentiary Canon at Bradford Cathedral, where she immersed herself in interfaith work with the Muslim population of that city. She has published books, most recently *Why Rousseau was Wrong* in 2013.

Lucy Winkett is Rector of St James's Church Piccadilly. She contributes regularly to Radio 4's *Thought for the Day* and is the author of *Our Sound is our Wound* (Continuum 2010). She combines parish ministry with chairing an educational trust and running an all-through Church of England Academy, including a project for children on the autistic spectrum. Until 2010, she was Canon Precentor of St Paul's Cathedral.

Samuel Wells is Vicar of St Martin in the Fields, London, and Visiting Professor of Christian Ethics at King's College, London. He is the author of a number of acclaimed books; his most recent titles are *What Anglicans Believe, Crafting Prayers for Public Worship* and *Learning to Dream Again*. He was formerly Dean of the Chapel and Research Professor of Christian Ethics at Duke University, North Carolina.

About *Reflections for Lent*

Based on the *Common Worship Lectionary* readings for Morning Prayer, these daily reflections are designed to refresh and inspire times of personal prayer. The aim is to provide rich, contemporary and engaging insights into Scripture.

Each page lists the lectionary readings for the day, with the main psalms for that day highlighted in **bold**. The Collect of the day – either the *Common Worship* collect or the shorter additional collect – is also included.

For those using this book in conjunction with a service of Morning Prayer, the following conventions apply: a psalm printed in parentheses is omitted if it has been used as the opening canticle at that office; a psalm marked with an asterisk may be shortened if desired.

A short reflection is provided on either the Old or New Testament reading. Popular writers, experienced ministers, biblical scholars and theologians will be contributing to this series. They all bring their own emphases, enthusiasms and approaches to biblical interpretation to bear.

Regular users of Morning Prayer and *Time to Pray* (from *Common Worship: Daily Prayer*) and anyone who follows the lectionary for their regular Bible reading will benefit from the rich variety of traditions represented in these stimulating and accessible pieces.

The book also includes both a simple form of Common Worship: Morning Prayer (see pp. 48–49) and a short form of Night Prayer – also known as Compline – (see pp. 52–55), particularly for the benefit of those readers who are new to the habit of the Daily Office or for any reader while travelling.

Making a habit of Lent

It's often said that life is about choices. But a life based on perpetual choice would be a nightmare. To avoid the tyranny of having to make perpetual choices, we develop habits. The point about habits is to develop good ones. That's what Lent is about. Here are the six most important ones.

- **Habit number one: look inside your heart.**
  Examine yourself. Find inside yourself some things that shouldn't be there. If they're hard to extract, get some help. Name them by sitting or kneeling down with a trusted friend or pastor, and just say, 'These things shouldn't be there. Please help me let God take them away.' Self-examination isn't just about finding things that shouldn't be there. It's also about finding things that are there but have been neglected. That's sometimes where vocation begins. Look inside your heart. Do it. Make a habit of it.

- **Habit number two: pray.**
  Don't get in a pickle about whether to pray with a book or just freestyle: do both. Once a day each. Simple as that. Think about the way you shop. Sometimes I shop with a list; sometimes not. Sometimes it's a pleasure; sometimes it's a necessity; sometimes it's a pain. Sometimes I go with someone else, or even help someone else to go; sometimes I go on my own. Sometimes it's about big things; sometimes it's about little things. Sometimes I really think carefully about it, and check through a kind of recipe list; sometimes I just do it, and realize later what I've forgotten. Prayer's just as varied. Just do it. Make a habit of it.

- **Habit number three: fast.**
  Fasting is about toughening yourself up so you don't go all pathetic at the first smell or sight of something sweet or tasty. It's about making yourself someone to be reckoned with and not a pushover. Make a pattern of life so you don't just drift to the mobile phone or email or internet as a transitional object. Stand in solidarity with those who don't get to choose. If you can't give up a single meal, do you really care about global hunger? And learn how to be really hungry. Hungry for righteousness. Hungry for justice and peace. Hungry, fundamentally, for Easter – hungry for the resurrection only God can bring in Christ. Do it. Make a habit of it.

- **Habit number four: give money away.**

  'Ah,' you may say, 'I'm in a tight spot right now: I don't have any money.' Let me tell you now: there will never be a time in your life when you think it's a good time for giving money away. Try to tie your money to your prayers. Give money to something you believe in, and pray for the organisation you give money to. Just do it. Make a habit of it.

- **Habit number five: read the Bible.**

  Imagine you were going into a crowded airport to meet someone you were longing to see but weren't sure you'd recognize. And imagine you had a photo album of pictures that showed them in a thousand different activities. Wouldn't you study that photo album so you'd almost committed it to memory? That's what the Bible is – a series of portrayals of God, and we study it to get to know God better so we'll have no recognition problems in a crowd. Genesis has 50 chapters: you can almost do it in Lent. You can get through a couple of Paul's letters a week. There's a dozen minor prophets: read a couple a week. Find a nether region in the Bible, and go digging. Buy an accessible commentary and follow a few verses each day. Just do it. Make a habit of it.

- **Habit number six: repair broken relationships.**

  This is the last one and, for many people, the toughest. We've probably, many of us, got one big relationship that's all wrong – and maybe there's not a whole lot we can do about it. Maybe it's just a matter of keeping out of someone's way, if we've done them wrong, or trying to be civil, if they've hurt us. Now may not be the time to make things better. Now may not yet be God's time. But that doesn't mean we let all our other relationships get to that kind of place. Is there someone out there, a sibling, a rival, a long-time friend, a person who always felt inferior to you? Could you write that person a letter this Lent to say some things you've always appreciated about them but you've never told them? You can make it subtle. You can dress it up as something else. But could you see your way to that? And what about people whose names you don't know, people from whom you're estranged without ever having done the damage yourself? Could you make a new friend this Lent? Do it. Make a habit of it.

May you have a holy Lent, rooted and grounded in love.

Samuel Wells

The importance of daily prayer

Daily prayer is a way of sustaining that most special of all relationships. It helps if we want to pray, but it can be sufficient to want to want to pray, or even to want to want to want to pray! The direction of the heart is what matters, not its achievements. Gradually we are shaped and changed by the practice of daily prayer. Apprentices in prayer never graduate, but we become a little bit more the people God wants us to be.

Prayer isn't a technique; it's a relationship, and it starts in the most ordinary, instinctive reactions to everyday life:

- **Gratitude**: good things are always happening to us, however small.
- **Wonder**: we often see amazing things in nature and in people but pass them by.
- **Need**: we bump into scores of needs every day.
- **Sorrow**: we mess up.

Prayer is taking those instincts and stretching them out before God. The rules then are: start small, stay natural, be honest.

Here are four ways of putting some structure around daily prayer.

1 **The Quiet Time**. This is the classic way of reading a passage of the Bible, using Bible reading reflections like those in this book, and then praying naturally about the way the passage has struck you, taking to God the questions, resolutions, hopes, fears and other responses that have arisen within you.

2 **The Daily Office**. This is a structured way of reading Scripture and psalms, and praying for individuals, the world, the day ahead, etc. It keeps us anchored in the Lectionary, the basic reading of the Church, and so ensures that we engage with the breadth of Scripture, rather than just with our favourite passages. It also puts us in living touch with countless others around the world who are doing something similar. There is a simple form of Morning Prayer on pages 48–9 of this book and a form of Night Prayer (Compline) on pages 52–5. Fuller forms can be found in *Common Worship: Daily Prayer.*

3 **Holy Reading**. Also known as *Lectio Divina*, this is a tried and trusted way of feeding and meditating on the Bible, described more fully on pages 6–7 of this book. In essence, here is how it is done:

- *Read:* Read the passage slowly until a phrase catches your attention.
- *Reflect:* Chew the phrase carefully, drawing the goodness out of it.
- *Respond:* Pray about the thoughts and feelings that have surfaced in you.
- *Rest:* You may want to rest in silence for a while.
- *Repeat:* Carry on with the passage ...

4 **Silence**. In our distracted culture some people are drawn more to silence than to words. This will involve *centring* (hunkering down), *focusing* on a short biblical phrase (e.g. 'Come, Holy Spirit'), *waiting* (repeating the phrase as necessary), and *ending* (perhaps with the Lord's Prayer). The length of time is irrelevant.

There are, of course, as many ways of praying as there are people to pray. There are no right or wrong ways to pray. 'Pray as you can, not as you can't', is wise advice. The most important thing is to make sure there is sufficient structure to keep prayer going when it's a struggle as well as when it's a joy. Prayer is too important to leave to chance.

+John Pritchard

Lectio Divina – a way of reading the Bible

Lectio Divina is a contemplative way of reading the Bible. It dates back to the early centuries of the Christian Church and was established as a monastic practice by Benedict in the sixth century. It is a way of praying the Scriptures that leads us deeper into God's word. We slow down. We read a short passage more than once. We chew it over slowly and carefully. We savour it. Scripture begins to speak to us in a new way. It speaks to us personally, and aids that union we have with God through Christ, who is himself the Living Word.

Make sure you are sitting comfortably. Breathe slowly and deeply. Ask God to speak to you through the passage that you are about to read.

This way of praying starts with our silence. We often make the mistake of thinking prayer is about what we say to God. It is actually the other way round. God wants to speak to us. He will do this through the Scriptures. So don't worry about what to say. Don't worry if nothing jumps out at you at first. God is patient. He will wait for the opportunity to get in. He will give you a word and lead you to understand its meaning for you today.

First reading: Listen

As you read the passage listen for a word or phrase that attracts you. Allow it to arise from the passage as if it is God's word for you today. Sit in silence repeating the word or phrase in your head.

Then say the word or phrase aloud.

Second reading: Ponder

As you read the passage again, ask how this word or phrase speaks to your life and why it has connected with you. Ponder it carefully. Don't worry if you get distracted – it may be part of your response to offer to God. Sit in silence and then frame a single sentence that begins to say aloud what this word or phrase says to you.

Third reading: Pray

As you read the passage for the last time, ask what Christ is calling from you. What is it that you need to do or consider or relinquish or take on as a result of what God is saying to you in this word or phrase? In the silence that follows the reading, pray for the grace of the Spirit to plant this word in your heart.

If you are in a group, talk for a few minutes and pray with each other.

If you are on your own, speak your prayer to God either aloud or in the silence of your heart.

If there is time, you may even want to read the passage a fourth time, and then end with the same silence before God with which you began.

+Stephen Cottrell

Wednesday 18 February

Ash Wednesday

Psalm **38**
Daniel 9.3-6, 17-19
1 Timothy 6.6-19

Daniel 9.3-6, 17-19

'For your own sake, O my God' (v. 19)

Daniel's cry is one of real desperation. As if not only he, but the whole city of God, is sinking in quicksand. Floundering is of no avail; no good to clutch at the straws of human righteousness and self-justification. The imperatives tumble over each other. Listen! Let your face shine upon us! Incline your ear! Open your eyes! Forgive! Do not delay! This is an urgent, wholehearted appeal to the mercy of God to save the city and people who bear God's name.

Anyone who suffers stress, or anxiety, or panic attacks knows the reality of this – how you feel like the foundations of life are no longer there. The more you try to find a secure foothold, the more shaky your hold on your life becomes. When the foundations are undermined, there seems nowhere to turn to escape. The more you struggle, the deeper you go.

It is Ash Wednesday today – a day on which to take seriously the reality of our utter dependence upon God. A day on which to remember how lost we are when we rely upon our own merit and virtue – how quickly things turn to dust and ashes in our hands without the grace of God sustaining and leading us. Let us pray today for a deepened sense of God's grace throughout the days of Lent ahead, so we come to know more clearly and dearly, and nearly, that sustaining love. Without it, we are already the dust to which we shall return. But not yet, for God's sake.

COLLECT

Almighty and everlasting God,
you hate nothing that you have made
and forgive the sins of all those who are penitent:
create and make in us new and contrite hearts
that we, worthily lamenting our sins
and acknowledging our wretchedness,
may receive from you, the God of all mercy,
perfect remission and forgiveness;
through Jesus Christ your Son our Lord,
who is alive and reigns with you,
in the unity of the Holy Spirit,
one God, now and for ever.

Psalms **77** *or* 56, **57** (63*)
Jeremiah 2.14-32
John 4.1-26

Jeremiah 2.14-32

'We are free, we will come to you no more' (v.31)

Freedom is largely understood today as freedom from constraint. This is freedom towards self-actualization, self-realization. When I'm unconstrained by any commitment to others, I can flourish, fulfil my potential, become what I am – so the mantra goes. The Lord God says: 'For long ago you broke your yoke and burst your bonds, and you said, "I will not serve!"' (v.20). This idea of freedom is obviously as old as the hills, for here it is, alive and kicking, among Jeremiah's contemporaries.

Such freedom, though, leads only to slavery. The sarcasm of the Lord is deftly directed towards a people that has already been rescued from slavery and oppression. And here they are, squandering the gift of freedom and exchanging it for another slavery, this time to lusts and passions, to self-indulgence. No freedom here.

St Augustine reminds us that we find perfect freedom in service. Service – that word turns up in so many contexts in today's world: in a game of tennis, in animal mating, in the armed forces, in actions done to benefit others, in the worship offered to God. However it is used, it's a relational word: service is something offered *by* one *to* another. No room here for that freefall away from responsibility that Jeremiah rails against! Perfect freedom comes when we tie ourselves in to the society of others, the society of God.

Holy God,
our lives are laid open before you:
rescue us from the chaos of sin
and through the death of your Son
bring us healing and make us whole
in Jesus Christ our Lord.

COLLECT

Friday 20 February

Jeremiah 3.6-22

'And I thought you would call me, My Father' (v.19)

The description of the people swings back and forth between the faithless whore and the children, continuing the lament of God at the betrayal of Israel. There is real tenderness here: a parent calling out for the lost child, hearing the plaintive weeping on the bare heights. There is also a yearning for reconciliation, for a coming-together of those who are estranged.

The Lord God is revealed as 'My Father', crying out for restored relationship: a Father who shows love with all the pain and loss of the rejected, who expresses the intimacy of the closest of any human relationship. Tender are the words; for though God has every right to wrath, yet what is here is the poignant calling for the acknowledgement of guilt so forgiveness can freely flow.

It's hard to forgive when we are wronged, when others betray us. The brilliance of C. S. Lewis' allegorical tale *The Great Divorce* lies in his description of those people who are trapped in their inability to forgive, who cannot be free of bitterness and recrimination, or of the selfish desire to control others and to manipulate. Hell is turning away from God into ever more distant solipsistic atomism where such faithlessness becomes habitual. 'My Father' waits as any parent waits through the night for the return of the adolescent. The parent who says, again and again, 'I thought you would call me'.

COLLECT

Almighty and everlasting God,
you hate nothing that you have made
and forgive the sins of all those who are penitent:
create and make in us new and contrite hearts
that we, worthily lamenting our sins
and acknowledging our wretchedness,
may receive from you, the God of all mercy,
perfect remission and forgiveness;
through Jesus Christ your Son our Lord,
who is alive and reigns with you,
in the unity of the Holy Spirit,
one God, now and for ever.

Psalm **71** or **68**
Jeremiah 4.1-18
John 4.43-end

Jeremiah 4.1-18

'O Jerusalem, wash your heart clean of wickedness' (v.14)

'Almighty God, unto whom all hearts be open, all desires known.' So begins the Collect for Purity in the Anglican liturgy. To come before God in worship requires open hearts, pure of any distraction or corruption, ready to receive the God of light and love. A heart that is filled with anger or bitterness, or is preoccupied with pornographic imagers and dirty secrets – such a heart needs to be transformed.

Or perhaps the heart is troubled and struggling, broken perhaps by loss. Perhaps it is beating irregularly – too quickly, too slowly. Full of disease or ill at ease through stress. Experiencing palpitations. Expressing with physical symptoms things that might be wrong in life.

John Donne talked, in one of his poems written at Montgomery Castle, of a 'naked thinking heart' – a heart open and undefended, a heart active in thought and feeling. Psalm 51 talks of 'a broken and contrite heart', which God will not despise (Psalm 51.17). Throughout the ages, the heart has symbolized the centre of life, of motivation, of response and responsibility.

Hardness of heart brings its own reward. For the city of Jerusalem it was the threat of war from the North, the boiling pot spilling over, bringing destruction, cleansing the heart of its wickedness, whether it liked it or not. How much better a heart responsive to God's love – a heart of flesh, not of stone.

Holy God,
our lives are laid open before you:
rescue us from the chaos of sin
and through the death of your Son
bring us healing and make us whole
in Jesus Christ our Lord.

COLLECT

Jeremiah 4.19-end

'I looked … there was no one at all' (v.25)

The pictures we have of prophets in our minds are very often a bit of a stereotype: an old man with a beard, a venerable figure with a powerful pen and ascetic lifestyle. Jeremiah, however, is young and, as we read later in this book, he has the word of God like 'a burning fire shut up in my bones' (Jeremiah 20.9). Over the next few days we will be seared by these flames: Jeremiah is unsparing, uncompromising and makes for difficult reading. Here, his anguish is plain because he anticipates the invading army moving towards beloved Jerusalem. The political is personal as Jeremiah feels personally the fear and desperation of approaching disaster. The intimacy of Jeremiah's metaphors is striking and moving: death is close, as close as an invading soldier drawing back the drapes of his bedroom (v.20). Death is certain and imminent.

For us at these centuries' distance, it might be hard to engage with this heightened language and energetic desperation. But Jeremiah teaches us a depth of personal involvement that is characteristic of him and leaves us with the question: what impact do broader political realities have on our own faith? Many of us receive information through the news while sitting in our own living rooms, alone or in small groups. One possible exercise is to take one news story and engage with it ourselves even if it is sending a letter or giving some money.

Jeremiah 5.1-19

'How can I pardon you?' (v.7)

Throughout this week, the lament for Jerusalem and the impending destruction is the theme. It's worth noting the ways that Jeremiah tries to communicate the urgency of all this; to have this kind of desperation and depth of agony written into the Scriptures is a theological reflection in itself. Jeremiah is employing every ounce of his linguistic capability in the service of convincing his readers that this situation is serious, and it is getting worse by the hour.

The poetic theme in this passage is that of a lawsuit. There are two indictments: first against the poor themselves, and then against the powerful. There are echoes of Genesis here, where the search was for enough righteous people so that Sodom would be saved. Here, the threshold is lower; Jeremiah is called to search for just one person, not ten as Abraham did (Genesis 18.32). These are the depths to which Jerusalem has fallen. And the completeness of the condemnation is alarming; not one person among the poor or the powerful is found, and so pardon is simply not possible.

The problem is not degeneracy per se, but what Jeremiah calls stubbornness, cynicism and self-sufficiency. In modern terms, this could be described as a sort of 'functional atheism', an assumption that if things are going to change (even in Church communities) then it is up to us alone to make this happen. We often live and work as if God didn't exist, even while praying, meeting and planning the future.

Heavenly Father,
your Son battled with the powers of darkness,
and grew closer to you in the desert:
help us to use these days to grow in wisdom and prayer
that we may witness to your saving love
in Jesus Christ our Lord.

COLLECT

13

Wednesday 25 February

Jeremiah 5.20-end

'... though the waves toss, they cannot prevail' (v.22)

After the indictments of yesterday, now come the poetic motifs of judgement and sentence. Jeremiah is still in his metaphorical law court. The indictments are clear: stubbornness and self-reliance. There is a beauty here, though, despite the strong condemnatory language. Jeremiah combines the dismissal of the people (they have turned aside and gone away) with a tender and evocative description of what God has done, how God has created the world, freely given to the people who have rejected their God. The rather delicate way in which he points out that the sand is a barrier for the sea to protect the people (v.22) – a barrier 'perpetual' so that however stormy the sea, the people will be sheltered – is moving.

In verse 29, God is hurt by the contrast between all the kindnesses of nature heaped upon the people and the way in which they simply don't see or hear with what gifts they are surrounded. This is powerful and arguably recognisable in a contemporary discussion about ecological disaster and the hubris of humanity who believe that whatever they do, the natural world will always be there. Jeremiah is pointing his readers to notice, to experience, to understand that they are living in a context of gifts. For his audience, as for us today, this surely means nothing less than accepting the gifted context in which we live and, in response, living less self-centredly and more thankfully for everything we receive.

COLLECT

Almighty God,
whose Son Jesus Christ fasted forty days in the wilderness,
and was tempted as we are, yet without sin:
give us grace to discipline ourselves in obedience to your Spirit;
and, as you know our weakness,
so may we know your power to save;
through Jesus Christ your Son our Lord,
who is alive and reigns with you,
in the unity of the Holy Spirit,
one God, now and for ever.

Psalms **42**, 43 *or* **78**.1-39*
Jeremiah 6.9-21
John 6.1-15

Jeremiah 6.9-21

'... ancient paths, where the good way lies' (v.16)

The main metaphor employed by Jeremiah to illustrate the stubbornness of people is to say that they can't hear or are not listening. There is a sense of people living their lives while wilfully ignoring the presence of God around and among them. Again the structure of indictment–judgement–sentence is used by Jeremiah to try to show the consequences of their actions. There is a completeness again in his description of the population; old and young together (v.11) are all living as if God is not there, not trying to communicate with the people. And this time, there is an invitation to the people so that they know what they have to do (from verse 16 onwards).

For modern readers, we shouldn't mistake this invitation. The 'ancient paths' are not synonymous with 'the good old days'. The ancient paths are, he says, where the 'good way lies', reviving a radical and dangerous memory of the time where God's justice and mercy infused human society and all complacency was challenged.

In the final few verses Jeremiah plays with the symbols of paths, crossroads and stumbling blocks, the ancient words whose echoes we hear centuries later when Paul uses the same language to describe Jesus himself (e.g. 1 Corinthians 1.23). It seems that the people are on a journey, walking towards the crossroads where the choices will be hard and the perils of falling more and more evident.

Heavenly Father,
your Son battled with the powers of darkness,
and grew closer to you in the desert:
help us to use these days to grow in wisdom and prayer
that we may witness to your saving love
in Jesus Christ our Lord.

COLLECT

15

Jeremiah 6.22-end

'... a refiner among my people' (v.27)

Vivid and noisy metaphors make this tumultuous passage all the more powerful in its announcement of doom for Jerusalem. The roaring sea, the thundering of horses' hooves, the clashing of military equipment leads Jeremiah to say that 'we have heard news of them' (v.24). Unlike the stubborn-hearted people who can't hear God, what they can hear now are the noises of impending destruction. And their response is one of despair, anguish, helplessness.

Within this helpless and hopeless situation, the people react by lamenting. The depth of their despair is as strong as if their only child had been killed. And in the midst of all this, Jeremiah makes a comment about his own place, his own vocation: he is a tester and a refiner. However, the action he is taking – of refining – is futile, 'for the wicked are not removed' (v.29). Yet still he speaks out; still he calls for lament and repentance.

This is another instance of Jeremiah's mixing of the personal and political. The portentous public events – the impending invasion and destruction of Jerusalem – are intimate to Jeremiah and his own purpose and vocation. Even though he identifies the uselessness of his witness, it is still his calling somehow to continue to find ways to say what he has to say. The irony is that even what he identified as futile words finds meaning and power for us today, centuries later. There seems therefore to be meaning in raising our own voices against injustice even when it seems hopeless or purposeless. There seems to be meaning in the protest itself, in the very act of speaking out, regardless of perceived successes or failures in achieving change in our lifetime.

Almighty God,
whose Son Jesus Christ fasted forty days in the wilderness,
and was tempted as we are, yet without sin:
give us grace to discipline ourselves in obedience to your Spirit;
and, as you know our weakness,
so may we know your power to save;
through Jesus Christ your Son our Lord,
who is alive and reigns with you,
in the unity of the Holy Spirit,
one God, now and for ever.

Jeremiah 7.1-20

'I will not hear you ...' (v.16)

At the beginning of chapter seven, we start reading what is known as Jeremiah's 'temple sermon'. It is a strongly worded statement of the main themes of Jeremiah's prophecy, which brings him into dispute with the temple ideology on which the state relied. What is striking is that Jeremiah is called to proclaim this challenge 'in the gate of the Lord's house' (v.2) – in the very temple itself. Jeremiah mocks the repetition of temple theology with its assumption of preservation of the status quo. He challenges any unthinking reliance on repetitious and banal liturgy (v.4).

This is strong teaching for us too. Jeremiah is excoriating about those who ignore the link between prayer and action. Turning up for worship while acting unjustly during the rest of the week is a hypocrisy too far for this prophet, and his critique is without qualification. In his own day, it was the oppression of orphans and widows (those most economically and socially disadvantaged) that delegitimized the repetitious prayers. For contemporary Christians, there will be a thousand examples of wasteful or competitive living that is dissonant with the freely given, grace-filled love of God in Christ. Even worse, Jeremiah claims, there is no shame among the people for the gap between their liturgy and their ethics. The searing question of verse 11, to Christian ears, will be familiar as Jesus of Nazareth raged centuries later in the spirit of Jeremiah, accusing the temple of harbouring those who would act unjustly towards the poor.

From verse 16, Jeremiah reveals what God is saying to him personally, instructing him not to pray for this people or to raise his voice in support of them. The condemnation is complete. The utterness of the oracle is overwhelming. Jeremiah is truly a voice for all those who despair at the world in which we live.

Heavenly Father,
your Son battled with the powers of darkness,
and grew closer to you in the desert:
help us to use these days to grow in wisdom and prayer
that we may witness to your saving love
in Jesus Christ our Lord.

COLLECT

Monday 2 March

Jeremiah 7.21-end

'... the days are surely coming' (v.32)

The temple sermon continues, and Jeremiah moves from criticizing the repetitive words of the liturgy to the gap he sees between liturgical action and the ethics of everyday life. Not only are the words empty and futile when they are not matched up with the actions of the people; now the ritual action and sacrifices are not authentic either.

There is a ruthlessness about Jeremiah's determination to leave nothing unsaid, nothing unscrutinized. Again all that is required of the people is that they listen, but this seems to be impossible for the ones who have 'stiffened their necks' (v.26). In typical Jeremiah style, it is not just hearing that he advocates, but listening, which implies an attentiveness, a willingness to be addressed by God, an openness to being shaped by the will of God that is more than simply hearing what is said.

The contrast is clear and is as contemporary as it is ancient. The opposite of attentiveness to God is living under the delusion of autonomy and self-sufficiency. Perhaps it is simply part of the human condition to live with the tension between a proper self-confidence as a child of God and the recognition that we are utterly dependent too: our willingness to be ready to be 'unmade' by God. Somehow cultivating in ourselves the courage even to ask for this is what Jeremiah is describing; nothing less will do.

Almighty God,
you show to those who are in error the light of your truth,
that they may return to the way of righteousness:
grant to all those who are admitted
    into the fellowship of Christ's religion,
that they may reject those things
    that are contrary to their profession,
and follow all such things as are agreeable to the same;
through our Lord Jesus Christ,
who is alive and reigns with you,
in the unity of the Holy Spirit,
one God, now and for ever.

Jeremiah 8.1-15

'... saying "Peace, peace", when there is no peace' (v.11)

While we might have got used to the extreme nature of some of Jeremiah's language and images, this chapter begins with something pretty shocking. Having condemned without qualification the ritual words and practices in the temple and having described the terror about to befall the people in the imminent invasion and destruction of the city by marauding troops, now Jeremiah says that not only is the present and the future subject to God's judgement, but the past is too. Those bones that have been laid to rest with honour, ritual and respect in the past will themselves now be dishonoured. Even the past acts of decency are now jeopardized by the present refusal of the people to be attentive to God.

Jeremiah is making a challenging point about time here: it is as if there is no time, or at least no progression in time, when it comes to considering the presence of God in relationship with the people. This is a profound reflection for today. It is a version of the reflection Jesus makes when he implores the crowd not to worry about tomorrow or yesterday because today has enough worries of its own. It's as if *now* is what there is and so now, today, is what matters. It won't stop us reflecting on the past or planning for the future, but the urgency of Jeremiah tells us that the time when it's even possible to be as deeply attentive to God as we should is right now, here where we are today.

Almighty God,
by the prayer and discipline of Lent
may we enter into the mystery of Christ's sufferings,
and by following in his Way
come to share in his glory;
through Jesus Christ our Lord.

COLLECT

Psalm **35** *or* **119.105-128**
Jeremiah 8.18 – 9.11
John 6.60-end

Jeremiah 8.18 – 9.11

'... no balm in Gilead' (8.22)

The tone moves in this passage from the legal indictments, judgements and sentences of the previous chapters to a more tragic vocabulary of illness, pain, grief and death. These verses contain a lament – not only Jeremiah's lament but the lament of the Lord. The insertion of the phrase 'says the Lord' (8.17) ensures that we, as readers, understand this is not just Jeremiah who weeps for the people; we are witnessing the grief of God. It is grief such as that of a parent for a sick child; somehow the pain of the child becomes the pain of the parent (8.21). All that both can do is watch the disease take hold and do its worst on the body of the beloved child. We are told here of the Lord's rage, grief and despair; somehow the refusal of the people to repent has removed the power of God to save them. There are simply no more options left. The restatement of 'they do not know me' (9.3) highlights the isolation and desolation of God, pleading with the people to return to the one who has loved them from the beginning.

As with much of Jeremiah's prophecy, although it will have been said in a specific circumstance, the general underlying themes are universal and applicable to different situations in different centuries. We are left wondering what our lives look like to this pleading God, grief-stricken at the state of the world we have helped to create.

COLLECT

Almighty God,
you show to those who are in error the light of your truth,
that they may return to the way of righteousness:
grant to all those who are admitted
    into the fellowship of Christ's religion,
that they may reject those things
    that are contrary to their profession,
and follow all such things as are agreeable to the same;
through our Lord Jesus Christ,
who is alive and reigns with you,
in the unity of the Holy Spirit,
one God, now and for ever.

Thursday 5 March

Jeremiah 9.12-24

'... send for the skilled women to come' (v.17)

It might be something of a relief to find some verses in this passage that are not quite so emotive, not quite so freighted with fury and despair. It may be that these verses, as other passages, are written by a different writer, enlarging on and deepening the themes of the more passionate prophetic writer who has gone before. The themes of wisdom, understanding, interpretation of the law, are all here. Thoroughly contemporary instructions are found from verse 23, where the wealthy, the wise and the strong are directed not to boast about their accomplishments. There is only one way to deepen our delight, and that is to trust in God knowing that love, justice and righteousness are worth more than might and money.

The middle section calling on women to lament follows a profound tradition of female mourners, musicians, singers, asking the women to give voice to the uncomforted people and their uncomforted God. It gives something of a response to the perennial question of suffering in the world. Impossible to explain or understand, perhaps what we can do in the face of terrible cruelty is lament, raise our voices in protest, give expression to the wordless pain evoked in us by what we see sometimes on the news. It is a way of combating compassion fatigue, a way of remembering our deep connectedness as human beings with other people whose names we may never know, but whose distress we see.

Almighty God,
by the prayer and discipline of Lent
may we enter into the mystery of Christ's sufferings,
and by following in his Way
come to share in his glory;
through Jesus Christ our Lord.

COLLECT

Friday 6 March

Jeremiah 10.1-16

'... scarecrows in a cucumber field' (v.5)

The outpouring of contrasts continues between life lived by the people now and life as it could be lived if the people were close to the heart of God. The detail of how idols are constructed and built is compelling; we can almost hear the axe working on the trunk of the tree, and the decoration of the wood with precious metals fastened with hammer and nails. The most wonderful picture of a scarecrow in a cucumber field is perhaps the most derisory image Jeremiah can think of for the 'false gods' so beloved of the people. The scarecrow is a static, lifeless form that has to be carried about because it can't even walk, guarding cucumber crops, in contrast to the grieving heart of God, who, we are about to be reminded again, put the stars in the heavens and made the rivers and the mountains. The disparity couldn't be starker.

The critical faith issue for Jeremiah – as arguably for us today – is not atheism but idolatry. Jeremiah uses the Hebrew word *hebel* (vv.3,8,15) to describe these idols, meaning 'nothingness'. But the idols are not only lifeless and vacuous, they are economically valuable. They have some worth in worldly terms, but none before God. Food for thought for a contemporary culture that values wealth, and continues to spend money on building and decorating idols.

COLLECT

Almighty God,
you show to those who are in error the light of your truth,
that they may return to the way of righteousness:
grant to all those who are admitted
      into the fellowship of Christ's religion,
that they may reject those things
      that are contrary to their profession,
and follow all such things as are agreeable to the same;
through our Lord Jesus Christ,
who is alive and reigns with you,
in the unity of the Holy Spirit,
one God, now and for ever.

Saturday 7 March

Jeremiah 10.17-24

'Correct me, O Lord ...' (v.24)

Once again Jeremiah moves back to his reflections on the relationship between public calamity and private grief in the face of this calamity. The people are told to gather their possessions, to be ready, packed, to go into exile. It is an act of imagination; by describing the impending disaster in practical and personal terms of tents, children, forced journeys, the prophet is inviting the listening audience to imagine how they will feel when the political situation becomes real in their own lives.

Jeremiah identifies a failure of leadership as the main problem. The 'shepherds' (the kings) have failed their people, and what will inevitably follow is the exile of the people. The final two verses of this excerpt form a prayer that could easily be prayed as a personal prayer today. Jeremiah invites us to affirm what we suspect is true, although we don't live by it, that in the end, we human beings don't control our own lives; that the direction of our lives is determined by any number of things, and certainly not only by our decisions or by trying to align things and people to our will.

It is a dangerous prayer to ask for correction, but the theme of Jeremiah's teaching is about little else. The call is to attentiveness right now, in this present moment, because in a very real sense, there is nothing else. The call is to dare to ask to be shaped by God's love and correction, to learn to lament along with God over the stubbornness of our own hearts and the suffering of the people; and to live as if on tiptoe, to live as if the future is already here.

Almighty God,
by the prayer and discipline of Lent
may we enter into the mystery of Christ's sufferings,
and by following in his Way
come to share in his glory;
through Jesus Christ our Lord.

COLLECT

23

Psalms **5**, 7 *or* **98**, 99, 101
Jeremiah 11.1-17
John 7.37-52

Jeremiah 11.1-17

'... your gods have become as many as your towns' (v.13)

There is a strong tendency in human nature to homogenize things: to suppress difference. There is also a strong tendency to dissipate things: to over-accentuate difference.

Egypt, as this passage recalls, was an 'iron-smelter'. Just as a furnace reduces particular objects with their various shapes to one malleable liquid, so Egypt sought to crush the particular loves, commitments and beliefs of its subjects by asserting one great monolithic vision of what the empire stood for. No wonder that the brave and rebellious Hebrews learnt to prize particularity.

But, lifetimes later, in Jeremiah's day, their descendants in Judah risk going the other way, and losing all sense of the divine unity that makes and holds difference together. They have gods for every corner of life, every place. These gods are merely the expression of needs; they are idols that mirror the multiple human interests that generate them. Taken together they are incoherent and amount to nothing. There is no sum to the parts.

Jeremiah calls his people back to the one true God who neither suppresses difference nor is himself just one more differential among many. This God made the universe, with all its differences. He defends them from the smelter, but requires his people never to forget their ultimate source.

COLLECT

Almighty God,
whose most dear Son went not up to joy but first he suffered pain,
and entered not into glory before he was crucified:
mercifully grant that we, walking in the way of the cross,
may find it none other than the way of life and peace;
through Jesus Christ your Son our Lord,
who is alive and reigns with you,
in the unity of the Holy Spirit,
one God, now and for ever.

Psalms **6, 9** *or* **106*** (or 103)
Jeremiah 11.18 – 12.6
John 7.53 – 8.11

Jeremiah 11.18 – 12.6

'Why does the way of the guilty prosper?' (12.1)

This is one of the great questions of the Bible. It is echoed in the book of Job, and again in some of the Psalms. In Psalm 73, for example, the wicked initially appear invulnerable: 'All in vain I have kept my heart clean and washed my hands in innocence', says the Psalmist (Psalm 73.13). The wicked, meanwhile, simply 'increase in riches' (Psalm 73.12).

Here, in one of what are sometimes called Jeremiah's 'confessions', we see his human vulnerability and the personal burden of the prophetic task. He is attacked by those near to him, and he cannot see any evidence of God's judgement doing what it is meant to do in his situation. This sensitive and often isolated prophet, whose task fell to him so young, has what in Christian terms we might see as a Gethsemane experience.

The loneliness and endurance of the prophet are a challenge but may also be an encouragement in a world where there seems much unjust prosperity, and it is hard to speak out against it. The Psalmist in Psalm 73 learnt to see deeper only when he 'went into the sanctuary of God' (Psalm 73.17); there, he learnt to see that the wicked are in fact set in 'slippery places' (Psalm 73.18).

Like Jeremiah, who manages to stay in the way of faithfulness even when he is close to despair, Christians have found that it is in the worship of God that the real 'ends' of things are disclosed.

COLLECT

Eternal God,
give us insight
to discern your will for us,
to give up what harms us,
and to seek the perfection we are promised
in Jesus Christ our Lord.

Psalms **38** *or* 110, **111**, 112
Jeremiah 13.1-11
John 8.12-30

Jeremiah 13.1-11

'... the loincloth was ruined' (v. 7)

The High Priest of the Jerusalem temple had two sets of priestly vestments: the so-called 'Golden Garments' that were worn often throughout the year, and a set of four, unembroidered linen garments that were worn on one day in the year only, when he entered the Holy of Holies on the Day of Atonement. Their purity was to be uncompromised, so a new set was used every year.

Jeremiah, who was from a priestly family, would have known the symbolic significance of the loincloth he was asked to buy and wear. It was something that could have a holy purpose – something that could express the greatest purity, and the greatest intimacy with God (as the linen undergarment touched the very skin of the priest).

At God's instruction, he wears this garment – never washing it – until it is soiled, and thus tells the story of his people's failures in responding to their call to be pure. Soiled as they are, they will then be put away to moulder – in a terrible warning of exile yet to come.

Like Adam and Eve hiding from God, or the seed in Jesus' parable that falls on rocky ground, this mouldering loincloth is a summons to all God's people to seek again the relationship with God in which we realize our highest calling: clinging to God.

And the first step in this clinging is to *listen*.

COLLECT

Almighty God,
whose most dear Son went not up to joy but first he suffered pain,
and entered not into glory before he was crucified:
mercifully grant that we, walking in the way of the cross,
may find it none other than the way of life and peace;
through Jesus Christ your Son our Lord,
who is alive and reigns with you,
in the unity of the Holy Spirit,
one God, now and for ever.

Psalms **56**, 57 *or* 113, **115**
Jeremiah 14
John 8.31-47

Jeremiah 14

'Because there has been no rain on the land the farmers are dismayed; they cover their heads' (v.4)

Why do the farmers adopt gestures of shame and penitence when faced with drought? Our supposedly sophisticated technological world looks askance at what – in most human cultures and epochs – has been the majority view, namely that the human, natural and spiritual realms are all interconnected. When something is 'out of joint' with one of them, then all three are affected – and sometimes disastrously. Shakespeare's characters often suggest that dark deeds are afoot, and the heavens displeased, by referring to unnatural occurrences and omens in the animal and plant kingdoms – as in *Macbeth*, when the horses eat one another on the night that King Duncan is assassinated.

Our confident, rational accounts of the world may do us service when they dispel superstition and unwarranted fear – and we may rightly be suspicious of claims that 'unnatural births', or lightning strikes, are signs of God's anger at our iniquity. But they can also be used to disguise from us some of the complex and culpable effects of what we do at the human level on the non-human world around us. And this is more a challenge than ever when the rapaciousness and automation of our agricultural, industrial and economic systems have their worst effects on places a long way away.

We do not easily perceive what ought often to make us cover our heads. Jeremiah's farmers and nobles may have a lesson to teach us, both in their sin, and also in their repentance.

Eternal God,
give us insight
to discern your will for us,
to give up what harms us,
and to seek the perfection we are promised
in Jesus Christ our Lord.

COLLECT

27

Friday 13 March

Psalm **22** *or* **139**
Jeremiah 15.10-end
John 8.48-end

Jeremiah 15.10-end

'Why is ... my wound incurable, refusing to be healed?' (v.18)

Jeremiah accuses God in the strongest terms here. 'Truly, you are to me like a deceitful brook, like waters that fail' (v.18). This is the voice of one who feels desperately abandoned.

The prophet at this low point recalls for me the figure of Philoctetes from Greek legend – a Greek warrior-hero and the inheritor of Heracles' bow and arrows. Philoctetes receives an incurable wound from a snake bite. It festers and stinks so much that his former comrades set him ashore on the island of Lemnos, where he is left utterly alone. Like Jeremiah, all his memories of the joys and delights of earlier times turn to ashes in his mouth.

Philoctetes will one day be saved by the utilitarian calculations of the Greek army in their war against Troy. After some years they have to return to Lemnos because they need the bow and arrows in their war effort – and after some debate (and the intercession of one man more compassionate than the others), Philoctetes is taken too, and healed, and returned to the fellowship of his people.

Jeremiah does not have to wait for his hope of salvation; it is neither delayed nor utilitarian. Assurance comes quickly from the God he is accusing, 'I am with you to save you and deliver you'. Not because God wants something he has, but because God wants *him*.

Almighty God,
whose most dear Son went not up to joy but first he suffered pain,
and entered not into glory before he was crucified:
mercifully grant that we, walking in the way of the cross,
may find it none other than the way of life and peace;
through Jesus Christ your Son our Lord,
who is alive and reigns with you,
in the unity of the Holy Spirit,
one God, now and for ever.

Lent

Psalms **31** *or* 120, **121**, 122
Jeremiah 16.10 – 17.4
John 9.1-17

Saturday 14 March

Jeremiah 16.10 – 17.4

'Your wealth and all your treasures I will give for spoil as the price of your sin' (17.3)

Sin has a price – every time. There is no sin without cost, and (as Dietrich Bonhoeffer reminded us), even if grace is offered to us for free, it is not cheap. This is because Christ bought it with his own blood.

The people of Judah, like Esau at the time of the patriarchs, are willing by their own act to lose the heritage that God gave them. This heritage will go to others, because – even if it was only momentarily (like Esau) – they cared more for something lesser.

Esau sold his birthright for a bowl of lentil stew, and he and his twin brother became sworn enemies as a consequence. But years later, Esau found new opportunities and new resources, and he and his brother would one day find a way back to one another and be reconciled.

God's fierce words of judgement against Judah for its worship of false gods are held in this passage within a greater promise that there will once again be a way back. The eyes of God that see the people's iniquity are the same eyes that watch over them when they are scattered. God will send hunters to rocky crevices in order to gather his beloved. Likewise (in a way that anticipates what Jesus will one day promise), he will send fishers to the deeps to draw his children back to him. The people's sin has a terrible cost, but the cost will not be the loss of God's regard for them.

Eternal God,
give us insight
to discern your will for us,
to give up what harms us,
and to seek the perfection we are promised
in Jesus Christ our Lord.

COLLECT

29

Monday 16 March   Psalms 70, **77** *or* 123, 124, 125, **126**
Jeremiah 17.5-18
John 9.18-end

Jeremiah 17.5-18

'Like the partridge hatching what it did not lay, so are all who amass wealth unjustly' (v.11)

Jeremiah's words speak into a situation of acute anxiety about what he calls 'the fatal day'. He wrestles with a feeling that his destiny could go either way, that so much is poised in the balance. The unjust are powerful. In the closing verses of this excerpt, Jeremiah reveals that he longs for healing, salvation, and refuge, but that he fears terror, shame, and disaster.

In situations of anxiety, Jeremiah's strategy is to think big. He sets the immediate sequence of events in the context of a far bigger story of ultimate origins and ultimate ends, for there is reason to hope that what was there right at the very beginning of time – God's 'glorious throne', 'shrine of our sanctuary' (v.12) – will endure to the end as well. In the world of unjust humans, there is no such endurance. Partridges hatch what they did not lay. But God lays the egg as well as hatching it; he made the world and will not forsake it. The inconstancy of human actions is bracketed by the constancy of God. And in this bigger picture, Jeremiah can reassure himself with words very reminiscent of another 'beginning' – the beginning of the Psalter: 'Happy are those who do not follow the advice of the wicked ... they are like trees planted by streams of water ... and their leaves do not wither' (Psalm 1.1,3).

COLLECT

Merciful Lord,
absolve your people from their offences,
that through your bountiful goodness
we may all be delivered from the chains of those sins
which by our frailty we have committed;
grant this, heavenly Father,
for Jesus Christ's sake, our blessed Lord and Saviour,
who is alive and reigns with you,
in the unity of the Holy Spirit,
one God, now and for ever.

Psalms 54, **79** *or* **132**, 133
Jeremiah 18.1-12
John 10.1-10

Jeremiah 18.1-12

'… he reworked it into another vessel' (v.4)

Like the potter who will not waste the clay he was using when a pot goes wrong, God too is willing to put it to a new purpose. God is a recycling God.

The language of God's infinite resourcefulness and responsiveness can seem very apt here, and it helps us to understand that we are in a relationship with God in which there is reciprocity. The things we do – whether to repent or to resist God – have consequences for how God relates to us. God's intentions can appear to alter when we – like the pot – 'spoil'. God will devise a new strategy to deal with the failure. 'I will change my mind', says the voice of God in this passage (v.8). Another pot will be made.

But we ought not to be misled by this bold statement into thinking of God as fickle. Read the text closely, and it is clear that the apparent changeability of God is really the result of the changeability of human beings in relation to God's purposes. If we change for good, God will not enact a promised destruction, and if we change for bad, God will not deliver a promised blessing. In the realm of human action, we have room to move, and as we move it will be as though God moves with us. But the realm of human action in its entirety is nevertheless held within the divine potter's sure and unerring hands.

Merciful Lord,
you know our struggle to serve you:
when sin spoils our lives
and overshadows our hearts,
come to our aid
and turn us back to you again;
through Jesus Christ our Lord.

COLLECT

Wednesday 18 March

Jeremiah 18.13-end

'I will show them my back, not my face' (v.17)

These are dark words for God's people, and dark days for Jeremiah. The people here are cursed, both by God and his prophet, and, in return, the prophet is on the receiving end of the murderous hostility of the people.

Things seem too dire for even a glimmer of hope. But perhaps there is one – even in that most devastating of divine utterances, 'I will turn my back on you'. Jesus himself would speak like that to Simon Peter when he said 'Get behind me, Satan!' (Matthew 16.23). What you see from behind is the back of the one who has put you behind them. But you also see the back of one whom you *follow*. Being at someone's back can be a mark or an occasion of discipleship, and Simon Peter's discipleship most certainly did not end when Jesus turned his back on him. It was deepened.

Moses, too, was shown God's 'back', on Mount Sinai, as we hear in Exodus 33. This was not a curse – on the contrary it was a privilege. It was a means by which all the 'goodness of God' would come to him. Early Christian commentary read this episode as a sign that Moses was being made a very special sort of disciple.

Here, in Jeremiah's day, might it be that, within the curse that is being laid upon them, the people are at the same time being given another chance to follow? An invitation to change course and be changed?

COLLECT

Merciful Lord,
absolve your people from their offences,
that through your bountiful goodness
we may all be delivered from the chains of those sins
which by our frailty we have committed;
grant this, heavenly Father,
for Jesus Christ's sake, our blessed Lord and Saviour,
who is alive and reigns with you,
in the unity of the Holy Spirit,
one God, now and for ever.

Thursday 19 March

Joseph of Nazareth

Isaiah 11.1-10

'… the lion shall eat straw' (v.7)

In a world where genetic modification becomes more and more easy, and more and more widespread, we have rightly become nervous about the many ways in which we interfere with 'wild nature'. But it's something we have done for centuries, and continue to do even without the help of the latest scientific technology. Sometimes it will be to make our dogs more dangerous, sometimes less, depending what more or less self-serving need we have for such changes. Sometimes it will be to make our leeks bigger or our roses more fragrant.

Perhaps this vision of God's holy mountain seems like a travesty of wild nature in the service of a human dream. What sort of a lion eats straw? Wouldn't such a lion have lost its 'lion-ness' to such a degree that it hardly merits the name? But this may not be a prediction of what awaits lions at the end of time, so much as a proclamation of the ultimate invincibility of the peace which passes all understanding. It passes all understanding, so we need pictures like these to help us approach a conception of it. But it's a real peace nevertheless, and it is surely coming, just as it pre-existed the creation of the world and that world's fall. For it is the peace of *God*, and we look forward to it not in a genetically modified future so much as a messianically modified one. Lions will experience it in their own proper way, according to God's plans for them, as we will experience it in ours.

COLLECT

God our Father,
who from the family of your servant David
raised up Joseph the carpenter
to be the guardian of your incarnate Son
and husband of the Blessed Virgin Mary:
give us grace to follow him
in faithful obedience to your commands;
through Jesus Christ your Son our Lord,
who is alive and reigns with you,
in the unity of the Holy Spirit,
one God, now and for ever.

Friday 20 March

Jeremiah 19.14 – 20.6

'I am making you a terror to yourself' (20.4)

It is a common phrase: we are our own worst enemies. Horror films of various kinds have dramatized this: a beleaguered group of people barricade themselves in somewhere to escape a threat from beyond, but even with every hatch, door or window sealed and guarded, they still find themselves being picked off one by one – for the enemy is within.

We can easily become 'terrors to ourselves', acting in a way that seeks to keep danger away but finding we are that danger. What Pashhur the priest does to Jeremiah the prophet is unwittingly a form of self-harm, for God's priests ought not to suppress God's prophets. Jeremiah declares that what Pashhur has done to him will be done to Pashhur and the temple and city he cares about. All will be 'put in the stocks' (20.2); all will be placed in captivity; all will have their agency removed.

Pashhur may prompt us to examine what we try to suppress or exclude because of what we want to defend or preserve. It may be that the 'priest' in us is trying to shut up the prophetic voice of God in us. If so, we are doomed to failure, and we are our own worst enemies, for this voice cannot be kept at bay.

COLLECT

Merciful Lord,
absolve your people from their offences,
that through your bountiful goodness
we may all be delivered from the chains of those sins
which by our frailty we have committed;
grant this, heavenly Father,
for Jesus Christ's sake, our blessed Lord and Saviour,
who is alive and reigns with you,
in the unity of the Holy Spirit,
one God, now and for ever.

Psalm **32** *or* **147**
Jeremiah 20.7-end
John 11.17-27

Jeremiah 20.7-end

'Sing to the Lord! ... Cursed be the day on which I was born!'
(vv.13,14)

If there was ever an argument against proof texting from the Bible by citing only single verses or phrases, this is it. Within just a few verses, Jeremiah makes these two bizarrely discordant exclamations, one of praise and one of curse. What context can make sense of this discordance? Or what lesson can be learnt from it?

At one very immediate level, this conflict of two apparently incompatible feelings may work to reassure us that the Bible knows how all human beings feel a good deal of the time. We feel complicated; our feelings seem to conflict. Jeremiah gives permission to voice these conflicts to God, which is a lesson in how to pray. Prayer is not a tea party, and polite manners are not needed.

At another level, Jeremiah shows something profoundly challenging about the life of faith. We cannot live without God, but to live in obedience to him is to be tested. He experiences the paradox of a situation where he blames God for making him speak, and at the same time cannot help but speak God's words. To speak makes him suffer, and not to speak makes him suffer. T.S. Eliot in his *Four Quartets* gives the same testimony in relation to the 'dove descending': the work of God's Spirit in us (as once in the prophets). 'Consumed by either fire or fire', we're faced with the choice of one pyre or another: living with the consequences of our sin or undergoing our redemption.

Merciful Lord,
you know our struggle to serve you:
when sin spoils our lives
and overshadows our hearts,
come to our aid
and turn us back to you again;
through Jesus Christ our Lord.

COLLECT

Monday 23 March

Psalms **73**, 121 *or* **1**, 2, 3
Jeremiah 21.1-10
John 11.28-44

Jeremiah 21.1-10

'… the way of life and the way of death' (v.8)

'Couldn't you just lighten it up a little, Jeremiah? Perhaps start with some good news?'

It's as well Jeremiah didn't have to get his oracles past any political spin-doctors, or even a Diocesan Press Officer! But of course he had to face something more draconian than that! We know he was imprisoned, mocked and tormented because he spoke truth to power, and even in the narrative here we can see that the king's 'enquiry' is really a loaded question, for the messenger feeds Jeremiah the answer the king wants to hear: 'perhaps the Lord will … make him withdraw from us' (v.2).

But Jeremiah pulls no punches and delivers not just 'an inconvenient truth' but a devastating, morale-sapping broadside: the king and the city face inevitable defeat. And yet, hidden in this death-dooming Jeremiad is a tiny, paradoxical strand of hope; the Lord is offering a way of life, running beside the way of death. The path of loss and exile will prove to be life-giving; it is staying where we are that will be deadly.

As we read through Jeremiah, we must imaginatively inhabit this paradox. Defeat, the loss of the familiar, exile in a strange culture (all familiar to Christians in our culture) may be a path to life. Passiontide is a good time to remember that.

COLLECT

Most merciful God,
who by the death and resurrection of your Son Jesus Christ
delivered and saved the world:
grant that by faith in him who suffered on the cross
we may triumph in the power of his victory;
through Jesus Christ your Son our Lord,
who is alive and reigns with you,
in the unity of the Holy Spirit,
one God, now and for ever.

Psalms **35**, 123 *or* **5**, 6 (8)
Jeremiah 22.1-5, 13-19
John 11.45-end

Jeremiah 22.1-5, 13-19

'I will build myself a spacious house' (v.14)

Perhaps this text ought to be smuggled into one of London's shiniest new buildings, the Shard. People opening the blinds in its 'large upper rooms' might find verses 13-14 engraved on the windows or inscribed on the panelling. This is not to say of course that any of the business conducted in that tallest of buildings is necessarily involved in 'dishonest gain' or 'practising oppression and violence' (v.17), but Jeremiah is right I think to point out that an obsession with image, with buildings that constitute a competitive representation of prestige and power, may well be a cover for fundamental moral failure and blindness. It is not 'competing in cedar' that makes us kings, but doing justice and righteousness.

Whatever we make of his architectural critique, Jeremiah's checklist of those who need special care and attention, to be given justice by the powerful, is as pertinent to our time as to his: those who have been robbed or defrauded – that might include the customers of payday loan companies; the alien – there is a message for our politicians and border-control agencies; the orphan and the widow – that is to say, those without family back-up or social support, who cannot meet their own needs and whose needs are not being met by others. There is a reminder that some form of effective social security is essential to a just society.

Gracious Father,
you gave up your Son
out of love for the world:
lead us to ponder the mysteries of his passion,
that we may know eternal peace
through the shedding of our Saviour's blood,
Jesus Christ our Lord.

COLLECT

Wednesday 25 March

Psalms 111, 113
1 Samuel 2.1-10
Romans 5.12-end

Annunciation of Our Lord to the Blessed Virgin Mary

1 Samuel 2.1-10

'… not by might' (v.9)

'Not by might shall a man prevail' (v.9, NASV). This is the kernel of Hannah's glorious song, the first draft of the Magnificat, a flash of insight shared across the centuries between two marginalized women, a lesson which the men of the world have yet to learn.

The feast of the Annunciation is a good day to read this text, which so radically subverts the proud talk, the arrogant mouths, 'the bows of the mighty' (v.4). Not only because Mary in her humility and fruitful obedience is the exact opposite of these, but because the way God himself took, in the incarnation, his way of defeating evil, was not our way. Not by might, not from above, not by smiting, but by choosing to share our weakness, by being woven in Mary's womb, into the weakness of the changing flesh. Not by the action of a tyrant, but by the passion of a Saviour, as we learn afresh this Passiontide, God defeats the darkness and renews life and light. And if he is to fulfil Hannah's prophecy, and lift the needy from the ash heap to make them sit with princes, then the Prince of Peace must come first with us to the dust and the ash heap. Today Mary helps him begin that task; next week we shall see him do it, shall hear him say 'It is finished'.

COLLECT

We beseech you, O Lord,
pour your grace into our hearts,
that as we have known the incarnation of your Son Jesus Christ
    by the message of an angel,
so by his cross and passion
we may be brought to the glory of his resurrection;
through Jesus Christ your Son our Lord,
who is alive and reigns with you,
in the unity of the Holy Spirit,
one God, now and for ever.

Psalms **40**, 125 *or* 14, **15**, 16
Jeremiah 23.9-32
John 12.12-19

Jeremiah 23.9-32

'My heart is broken within me' (v.9, RSV)

It is heart-breaking to believe in God. To believe in God in a broken world is to keep hope alive, but hope in a broken world is almost always hope deferred, and 'hope deferred makes the heart sick' (Proverbs 13.12). How much easier it is to have no expectations: is the land full of adulterers? It won't hurt as long as you don't believe in marriage. Are the prophets, the priests, the leaders in Church and nation sometimes corrupted and corrupting? Well, just give in to the cynicism and contempt of the times and you won't be disappointed.

What makes Jeremiah such compelling reading, even at his darkest, is that he won't give up or give in. He sees the corruption more clearly than anyone, but he persists in expecting better. He won't take the easy option or accept the second best: the false hopes, the lying dreams. 'My heart is broken within me and my bones shake', he tells us, but a broken heart is still a loving heart. For the same love that breaks it is the love that keeps it alive. And our Lord knows that too. 'My heart is broken and my bones shake' might be the words from the cross of one whose love for us will not be defeated by disappointment.

Most merciful God,
who by the death and resurrection of your Son Jesus Christ
delivered and saved the world:
grant that by faith in him who suffered on the cross
we may triumph in the power of his victory;
through Jesus Christ your Son our Lord,
who is alive and reigns with you,
in the unity of the Holy Spirit,
one God, now and for ever.

COLLECT

39

Friday 27 March

Psalms **22**, 126 *or* 17, **19**
Jeremiah 24
John 12.20-36*a*

Jeremiah 24

'Two baskets of figs' (v.1)

Kenneth Anger, the American experimental filmmaker, wrote an infamous and scandalmongering book called *Hollywood Babylon,* of which the *New York Times* said, 'here is a book without one single redeeming merit'. From Anger's book, to the lyrics of Bob Marley, it has become a commonplace to associate the shallow materialism and consumerism of our times with the 'Babylon' of the Jewish exile. It is not surprising that Christians too, struggling to keep alive the radical love of the gospel and the values of the kingdom in the midst of contemporary 'me-culture', should also think of themselves as Babylonian exiles.

But if so, then Jeremiah's vision should give us pause. It is not to Jerusalem but to Babylon that the Word comes. Not in Jerusalem, but in Babylon that we are to be given a new heart to know the Lord. We think we're in the good basket, but perhaps instead of pining for our 'Jerusalem', looking back nostalgically to the 'good old days' when churches were full and the gospel got a hearing on the public stage, we should instead be looking and listening closely to the Babylon around us. Are there stirrings of hope? Rumours of angels? Signs from the Lord in the music and the films? Should we look for any good in Hollywood-Babylon? I think Jeremiah says 'Yes!'

COLLECT

Most merciful God,
who by the death and resurrection of your Son Jesus Christ
delivered and saved the world:
grant that by faith in him who suffered on the cross
we may triumph in the power of his victory;
through Jesus Christ your Son our Lord,
who is alive and reigns with you,
in the unity of the Holy Spirit,
one God, now and for ever.

Psalms **23**, 127 *or* 20, 21, **23**
Jeremiah 25.1-14
John 12.36b-end

Jeremiah 25.1-14

'I have spoken persistently' (v.3)

In the world of the quick fix, of instant gratification, of sound bites, of a constant stream of new acts, new faces, new slogans, persistence is in short supply. Even had he trimmed his sails to the wind, Jeremiah would have been fortunate to have lasted 23 years on any contemporary 'media outlet'. The first sign of grey hair and he would have been gone.

And perhaps that's why his persistence, and the persistence of all the Scriptures, the quiet persistence of this Lectionary, is so rewarding. Disquieting too, of course – in the case of Jeremiah, sometimes very disquieting! But as the whole of Jeremiah's persistent and consistent message proclaims, we sometimes need unsettling; we need bad news and inconvenient truths before we can grasp and ask for the good news of salvation.

The persistence of this single prophetic message, from Jeremiah to Nelson Mandela, that all is not well, that we must turn from evil and wrongdoing, the very persistence of that message is itself a sign of the patience and the grace of God. However many times we may have decided, as individuals or as a nation, that we have finished with God, the persistence of the prophets is a sign that he has not yet finished with us.

Gracious Father,
you gave up your Son
out of love for the world:
lead us to ponder the mysteries of his passion,
that we may know eternal peace
through the shedding of our Saviour's blood,
Jesus Christ our Lord.

COLLECT

Monday 30 March

Monday of Holy Week

Psalm 41
Lamentations 1.1-12*a*
Luke 22.1-23

Luke 22.1-23

'... until the kingdom of God comes' (v.18)

Holy week compresses the contrasts and contradictions of life, holding them in terrible tension. Outer action meets inner truth, private agony becomes public spectacle, our deepest yearnings and our darkest dreads coalesce in the same experience. So this passage begins with political conspiracy, foreshadows personal betrayal, and yet sets these in the midst of intimate exchange – the poignant farewell of friends. And that farewell becomes a shared meal, both ritualized and spontaneous. Jesus transforms and renews the Passover. In breaking the bread and pouring the wine, he shows that *he* will not be passed over, that he chooses instead to be the lamb whose blood saves others. Even the symbols of those dreadful things that will be done to his body and blood are transformed into gift, into signs and tokens of love, 'I have eagerly desired this,' he says, 'to share this moment, this meal, this sacrament, the heart of who I am, with you.' Here is wounded Love bidding us welcome.

As we follow the dark events of this week, we should remember that Love has 'desired' this, that through the pain, he sees the joy set before him, his joy and ours, when we shall drink the fruit of the vine, new with him. Meanwhile we still hold these contradictions in tension 'until the kingdom of God comes'.

COLLECT

Almighty and everlasting God,
who in your tender love towards the human race
    sent your Son our Saviour Jesus Christ
to take upon him our flesh
and to suffer death upon the cross:
grant that we may follow the example of his patience and humility,
and also be made partakers of his resurrection;
through Jesus Christ your Son our Lord,
who is alive and reigns with you,
in the unity of the Holy Spirit,
one God, now and for ever.

Psalm 27
Lamentations 3.1-18
Luke 22.[24-38] 39-53

Luke 22. [24-38] 39-53

'He drew near to Jesus to kiss him' (v.47, RSV)

There is no betrayal without intimacy, no intimacy without the risk of betrayal. To love at all, to trust anyone, is to risk that undoing. If God in Christ is to take on our humanity, then he must take on this, this dreadful reversal, in which the kiss that could and should be the kiss of peace, the kiss of fellowship, becomes the kiss of treachery.

At this moment in the garden, Jesus not only takes in and experiences this worst of all the shocks that flesh is heir to, but also takes it on. He takes it on by showing that love does not have to be defeated or reversed by betrayal, that when our humanity is betrayed and abandoned by our own inhumanity, we are not abandoned by God. Peter, as we shall see tomorrow, is also a betrayer, but the Love that hangs on the cross hangs on to him, finds and restores him.

Peter remembered and hung on; Judas despaired and hanged himself. But perhaps one reason that Christ descended into hell was to find Judas and 'draw near to him', to find the Judas in us, and offer him the same chance to turn again that Peter eventually took, so that, even for Judas, the kiss of betrayal might be redeemed again by the kiss of peace.

True and humble king,
hailed by the crowd as Messiah:
grant us the faith to know you and love you,
that we may be found beside you
on the way of the cross,
which is the path of glory.

COLLECT

Wednesday 1 April

Wednesday of Holy Week

Psalm 102 [*or* 102.1-18]
Wisdom 1.16 – 2.1; 2.12–22
or Jeremiah 11.18-20
Luke 22.54-end

Luke 22.54-end

'Then Peter remembered' (v.61)

'Some dance to remember, some dance to forget.' That famous line from the Eagles' hit song 'Hotel California' speaks to the ambivalence of memory. We can be trapped in memories, and yet remembering can also be the key that sets us free. So it is with Peter. The cock crows and he remembers. First he remembers the prediction of his denial, the prediction he has so weakly fulfilled, and he weeps bitterly. He weeps because he remembers what high hopes and self-confidence he had; he weeps because he has failed himself and his friend; he weeps in shame and humiliation. But, thanks be to God, his memory does not stop there. If he is to have any hope, then today Peter must remember the words of Jesus we heard yesterday: 'when once you have turned back, strengthen your brothers' (Luke 22.32).

It is bitter to remember our failure, but to remember that Jesus knew and knows our failure, that he prays for us and loves us through it, that he still sees a role for us and a place in his kingdom, that he sees not only our fall but also our rising – that is to remember well, to remember deeply, to know, with Peter, what T. S. Eliot meant in the *Four Quartets* when he said: 'This is the use of memory: for liberation.'

COLLECT

Almighty and everlasting God,
who in your tender love towards the human race
    sent your Son our Saviour Jesus Christ
to take upon him our flesh
and to suffer death upon the cross:
grant that we may follow the example of his patience and humility,
and also be made partakers of his resurrection;
through Jesus Christ your Son our Lord,
who is alive and reigns with you,
in the unity of the Holy Spirit,
one God, now and for ever.

Psalms 42, 43
Leviticus 16.2-24
Luke 23.1-25

Luke 23.1-25

'Herod and Pilate became friends' (v.12)

Evil has its own twisted fellowship, and perversity has its own perverted communion. It is ironic that on this Maundy Thursday, the day we celebrate the founding of a true communion in and through the gift of Christ's love, we should have a reading that depicts a corrupt and corrupting political alliance founded on the rejection of that love.

Herod and Pilate were indeed 'at enmity'. They represented opposed powers and races, opposed philosophies and faiths, held in an uneasy stalemate that would soon give way to the appalling violence that destroyed Jerusalem in 70 AD. But here, these two cunning politicians, with their precarious and vainglorious hold on power, find common cause, and more than common cause. They had both in their own way recognized a truth in Jesus; they both failed its test and rejected its claims on them, and then both proceeded to pervert the course of justice. Those who have done dreadful deeds crave each other's company, for some horrors are too much to bear alone; they seek a mutual entrenchment, a co-dependency, a conspiracy against the repentance that might come upon them if they were alone. We see it in death squads, drug gangs, and paedophile rings, and we see it starting here between Herod and Pilate. But in the foot-washing ceremonies that will take place in countless churches today, we celebrate its opposite and antidote, the new commandment that founds true community.

God our Father,
you have invited us to share in the supper
which your Son gave to his Church
to proclaim his death until he comes:
may he nourish us by his presence,
and unite us in his love;
who is alive and reigns with you,
in the unity of the Holy Spirit,
one God, now and for ever.

COLLECT

45

Friday 3 April

Good Friday

Psalm 69
Genesis 22.1-18
John 19.38-end *or* Hebrews 10.1-10

Hebrews 10.1-10

'Once for all' (vv.2,10)

The whole of Hebrews, with its radical re-interpretation of temple sacrifice, its mystical glimpses of the mysteries of heaven, is summed up in these three little words: 'once for all'. Christ's self-offering once for all, in sacrifice on the cross and in glory in the garden, is the single event that gives shape and meaning to all other events.

Christians used to worry and dispute with one another about whether every Eucharist, in which we remember Christ's sacrifice on Good Friday, is a renewal of this one event, a mere remembrance of it, or a 'vain repetition' of it. But really there is no repetition, there is only this single event, and every celebration of communion, every remembrance of his sacrifice, every moment of conversion and renewal in our personal history or the history of our Church, is a doorway out of time back into this one all-changing, all-saving event.

Just as cosmologists refer to the 'Big Bang' as a 'singularity', a one-off event from which all other events unfold, one that lies behind all the other recurring events we observe in our universe, so we might think of Jesus' death 'once for all' on the cross as a little like that: a spiritual 'singularity', a founding event that underlies and informs everything else.

Some Christians like to put others to the test, saying: 'Can you name the day on which you were saved?' There can only ever be one answer to that question: 'I was saved on Good Friday.'

COLLECT

Almighty Father,
look with mercy on this your family
for which our Lord Jesus Christ was content to be betrayed
    and given up into the hands of sinners
    and to suffer death upon the cross;
who is alive and glorified with you and the Holy Spirit,
one God, now and for ever.

Psalm 142
Hosea 6.1-6
John 2.18-22

John 2.18-22

'The temple of his body' (v.21)

On the day after its destruction, when his body lies cold in the tomb, we contemplate the holiness of the body we have broken.

It took 46 years to build the temple in Jerusalem, but if we said it had taken 33 years to make the temple of Christ's body, we should be short of the mark. These intricate, intimate, precious and perilous estates we call our bodies were longer in the making than we can imagine. That 'fearful and wonderful' making goes back beyond the glimpses we get in Psalm 139 of God at work in the womb, back through the intricate lines of inheritance from forbears and ancestors, back through the evolution of species, through the first formation of the folded strands of life itself, back to the beginning of that mysterious nexus of embodied being to which we give the little name 'cosmos'.

That these strange, beautiful bodies, with their interweaving of interdependent systems, and their billion connections of the brain, should arise and be formed from the stuff of the world, the dust of the earth, is a mystery and miracle, which not only puts us in awe, but is hallowed by God, for he tells us in this passage that the body is a temple. Ours is the body he took by grace, laid down in love, and will raise in glory.

Grant, Lord,
that we who are baptized into the death
of your Son our Saviour Jesus Christ
may continually put to death our evil desires
and be buried with him;
and that through the grave and gate of death
we may pass to our joyful resurrection;
through his merits,
who died and was buried and rose again for us,
your Son Jesus Christ our Lord.

COLLECT

Morning Prayer – a simple form

O Lord, open our lips
and our mouth shall proclaim your praise.

A prayer of thanksgiving for Lent *(for Passiontide see p. 50)*

Blessed are you, Lord God of our salvation,
to you be glory and praise for ever.
In the darkness of our sin you have shone in our hearts
to give the light of the knowledge of the glory of God
in the face of Jesus Christ.
Open our eyes to acknowledge your presence,
that freed from the misery of sin and shame
we may grow into your likeness from glory to glory.
Blessed be God, Father, Son and Holy Spirit.
Blessed be God for ever.

Word of God

Psalmody *(the psalm or psalms listed for the day)*

**Glory to the Father and to the Son
and to the Holy Spirit;
as it was in the beginning is now:
and shall be for ever. Amen.**

Reading from Holy Scripture *(one or both of the passages set for the day)*

Reflection

The Benedictus (The Song of Zechariah) *(see opposite page)*

Prayers

Intercessions – a time of prayer for the day and its tasks, the world and its need, the church and her life.

The Collect for the Day

The Lord's Prayer *(see p. 51)*

Conclusion

A blessing or the Grace *(see p. 51)*, or a concluding response

Let us bless the Lord
Thanks be to God

Benedictus (The Song of Zechariah)

1 Blessed be the Lord the God of Israel, ◆
who has come to his people and set them free.

2 He has raised up for us a mighty Saviour, ◆
born of the house of his servant David.

3 Through his holy prophets God promised of old ◆
to save us from our enemies,
from the hands of all that hate us,

4 To show mercy to our ancestors, ◆
and to remember his holy covenant.

5 This was the oath God swore to our father Abraham: ◆
to set us free from the hands of our enemies,

6 Free to worship him without fear, ◆
holy and righteous in his sight
all the days of our life.

7 And you, child, shall be called the prophet of the Most High, ◆
for you will go before the Lord to prepare his way,

8 To give his people knowledge of salvation ◆
by the forgiveness of all their sins.

9 In the tender compassion of our God ◆
the dawn from on high shall break upon us,

10 To shine on those who dwell in darkness
and the shadow of death, ◆
and to guide our feet into the way of peace.

Luke 1.68-79

**Glory to the Father and to the Son
and to the Holy Spirit;
as it was in the beginning is now:
and shall be for ever. Amen.**

Seasonal Prayers of Thanksgiving

Passiontide

Blessed are you, Lord God of our salvation,
to you be praise and glory for ever.
As a man of sorrows and acquainted with grief
your only Son was lifted up
that he might draw the whole world to himself.
May we walk this day in the way of the cross
and always be ready to share its weight,
declaring your love for all the world.
Blessed be God, Father, Son and Holy Spirit.
Blessed be God for ever.

At Any Time

Blessed are you, creator of all,
to you be praise and glory for ever.
As your dawn renews the face of the earth
bringing light and life to all creation,
may we rejoice in this day you have made;
as we wake refreshed from the depths of sleep,
open our eyes to behold your presence
and strengthen our hands to do your will,
that the world may rejoice and give you praise.
Blessed be God, Father, Son and Holy Spirit.
Blessed be God for ever.

after Lancelot Andrewes (1626)

The Lord's Prayer and The Grace

Our Father in heaven,
hallowed be your name,
your kingdom come,
your will be done,
on earth as in heaven.
Give us today our daily bread.
Forgive us our sins
as we forgive those who sin against us.
Lead us not into temptation
but deliver us from evil.
For the kingdom, the power,
and the glory are yours
now and for ever.
Amen.

(or)

Our Father, who art in heaven,
hallowed be thy name;
thy kingdom come;
thy will be done;
on earth as it is in heaven.
Give us this day our daily bread.
And forgive us our trespasses,
as we forgive those who trespass against us.
And lead us not into temptation;
but deliver us from evil.
For thine is the kingdom,
the power and the glory,
for ever and ever.
Amen.

The grace of our Lord Jesus Christ,
and the love of God,
and the fellowship of the Holy Spirit,
be with us all evermore.
Amen.

An Order for Night Prayer (Compline)

Preparation

The Lord almighty grant us a quiet night and a perfect end.
Amen.

Our help is in the name of the Lord
who made heaven and earth.

A period of silence for reflection on the past day may follow.

The following or other suitable words of penitence may be used

**Most merciful God,
we confess to you,
before the whole company of heaven and one another,
that we have sinned in thought, word and deed
and in what we have failed to do.
Forgive us our sins,
heal us by your Spirit
and raise us to new life in Christ. Amen.**

O God, make speed to save us.
O Lord, make haste to help us.

**Glory to the Father and to the Son
and to the Holy Spirit;
as it was in the beginning is now
and shall be for ever. Amen.
Alleluia.**

The following or another suitable hymn may be sung

Before the ending of the day,
Creator of the world, we pray
That you, with steadfast love, would keep
Your watch around us while we sleep.

From evil dreams defend our sight,
From fears and terrors of the night;
Tread underfoot our deadly foe
That we no sinful thought may know.

O Father, that we ask be done
Through Jesus Christ, your only Son;
And Holy Spirit, by whose breath
Our souls are raised to life from death.

The Word of God

One or more of Psalms 4, 91 or 134 may be used.

Psalm 134

1   Come, bless the Lord, all you servants of the Lord, ◈
    you that by night stand in the house of the Lord.

2   Lift up your hands towards the sanctuary ◈
    and bless the Lord.

3   The Lord who made heaven and earth ◈
    give you blessing out of Zion.

**Glory to the Father and to the Son
and to the Holy Spirit;
as it was in the beginning is now
and shall be for ever. Amen.**

Scripture Reading

*One of the following short lessons or another suitable
passage is read*

You, O Lord, are in the midst of us and we are called by your
name; leave us not, O Lord our God.

Jeremiah 14.9

(or)

Be sober, be vigilant, because your adversary the devil is
prowling round like a roaring lion, seeking for someone
to devour. Resist him, strong in the faith.

1 Peter 5.8,9

(or)

The servants of the Lamb shall see the face of God, whose name
will be on their foreheads. There will be no more night: they will
not need the light of a lamp or the light of the sun, for God will
be their light, and they will reign for ever and ever.

Revelation 22.4,5

Into your hands, O Lord, I commend my spirit.
Into your hands, O Lord, I commend my spirit.
For you have redeemed me, Lord God of truth.
I commend my spirit.
Glory to the Father and to the Son
and to the Holy Spirit.
Into your hands, O Lord, I commend my spirit.

Or, in Easter

Into your hands, O Lord, I commend my spirit.
    Alleluia, alleluia.
Into your hands, O Lord, I commend my spirit.
    Alleluia, alleluia.
For you have redeemed me, Lord God of truth.
Alleluia, alleluia.
Glory to the Father and to the Son
and to the Holy Spirit.
Into your hands, O Lord, I commend my spirit.
    Alleluia, alleluia.

Keep me as the apple of your eye.
Hide me under the shadow of your wings.

Gospel Canticle

Nunc Dimittis (The Song of Simeon)

Save us, O Lord, while waking,
and guard us while sleeping,
that awake we may watch with Christ
and asleep may rest in peace.

1   Now, Lord, you let your servant go in peace:
    your word has been fulfilled.

2   My own eyes have seen the salvation
    which you have prepared in the sight of every people;

3   A light to reveal you to the nations
    and the glory of your people Israel.

Luke 2.29-32

Glory to the Father and to the Son
and to the Holy Spirit;
as it was in the beginning is now
and shall be for ever. Amen.

Save us, O Lord, while waking,
and guard us while sleeping,
that awake we may watch with Christ
and asleep may rest in peace.

Prayers

Intercessions and thanksgivings may be offered here.

The Collect

Visit this place, O Lord, we pray,
and drive far from it the snares of the enemy;
may your holy angels dwell with us and guard us in peace,
and may your blessing be always upon us;
through Jesus Christ our Lord.
Amen.

The Lord's Prayer (see p. 51) may be said.

The Conclusion

In peace we will lie down and sleep;
for you alone, Lord, make us dwell in safety.

Abide with us, Lord Jesus,
for the night is at hand and the day is now past.

As the night watch looks for the morning,
so do we look for you, O Christ.

[Come with the dawning of the day
and make yourself known in the breaking of the bread.]

The Lord bless us and watch over us;
the Lord make his face shine upon us and be gracious to us;
the Lord look kindly on us and give us peace.
Amen.

Love what you've read?

Why not consider using *Reflections for Daily Prayer* all year round? We also publish these Bible notes in an annual format, containing material for the entire church year.

The volume for the 2015/16 church year will be published in May 2015 and features contributions from a host of distinguished writers: Rosalind Brown, Gillian Cooper, Steven Croft, Andrew Davison, Maggi Dawn, Paula Gooder, Peter Graystone, Mary Gregory, Malcolm Guite, Emma Ineson, Jan McFarlane, Barbara Mosse, Mark Oakley, Martyn Percy, Ben Quash, Martyn Snow and Jane Williams.

Reflections for Daily Prayer:
Advent 2015 to the eve of Advent 2016

ISBN 978 0 7151 4457 2
£16.99
Available May 2015

Can't wait for next year?

You can still pick up this year's edition of *Reflections*, direct from us (see p. 58 for details of how to order) or from your local Christian bookshop.

Reflections for Daily Prayer:
Advent 2014 to the eve of Advent 2015

ISBN 978 0 7151 4366 7
£16.99 • Available Now

Reflections for Daily Prayer
App

Make Bible study and reflection a part of your routine wherever you go with the Reflections for Daily Prayer App for Apple and Android devices.

Download the app for free from the App Store (Apple devices) or Google Play (Android devices) and receive a week's worth of reflections free. Then purchase a monthly, three-monthly or annual subscription to receive up-to-date content.

App opens on that day's Church of England Bible reading notes

Scrolling or paging reading options

Additional simple morning prayer format

First daily readings free - then choose a monthly, quarterly or annual subscription

Resources for Daily Prayer

Common Worship: Daily Prayer

The official daily office of the Church of England,
Common Worship: Daily Prayer is a rich collection of
devotional material that will enable those wanting to
enrich their quiet times to develop
a regular pattern of prayer. It includes:

- Prayer During the Day
- Forms of Penitence
- Morning and Evening Prayer
- Night Prayer (Compline)
- Collects and Refrains
- Canticles
- Complete Psalter

896 pages • with 6 ribbons • 202 x 125mm

Hardback	978 0 7151 2199 3	**£22.50**
Soft cased	978 0 7151 2178 8	**£27.50**
Bonded leather	978 0 7151 2277 8	**£50.00**

Time to Pray

This compact, soft-case volume offers two simple,
shorter offices from *Common Worship: Daily Prayer*.
It is an ideal introduction to a more structured
personal devotional time, or can be used as a lighter,
portable daily office for those on the move.

Time to Pray includes:

- Prayer During the Day
  (for every day of the week)
- Night Prayer
- Selected Psalms

£12.99 • 112 pages • Soft case
ISBN 978 0 7151 2122 1